The Véronique
French Language

THE ULTIMATE FRENCH QUIZ BOOK FOR BEGINNER & INTERMEDIATE LEVELS

500 GRAMMAR PRACTICE QUESTIONS

By Véronique F. Courtois, MA, MS
The Sorbonne-Nouvelle, Paris III, France
Former Instructor, Tufts University &
Boston University, Massachusetts
The French Library in Boston, Massachusetts,
The Beverly Hills Lingual Institute, Beverly Hills, California,
The French Alliance of Los Angeles, California

ISBN 9780998080468

Dear Student of French,

This quiz book is intended for you if you are:

*A Francophile who studied French years ago and needs to refresh his/her French grammar skills.

*A high school or a university student taking a French class and seeking a quick general review before an exam.

These quiz questions are intended to help you assess the grammar points you need to master in order to pass your French tests or exams. Grammatical explanations are not included in this Quiz book as French grammar rules are widely available for free or for purchase online.

The more you practice these questions and review the corresponding material, the better prepared you'll be when sitting for your exams.

You can contact me through my Facebook Page:
www.facebook.com/VeroniqueFCourtoisBooks

Or my email address: **vfcfrenchtutoring@gmail.com**

Merci et bonne chance !
Véronique

LISTE DES CHAPITRES

INTRODUCTION: **Test d'évaluation** *vii*

CHAPITRE 1 : **Les verbes au présent : être, avoir, aller, pouvoir, vouloir** *1*

CHAPITRE 2 : **C'est, Il/Elle est, Il y a (les prépositions)** *6*

CHAPITRE 3 : **Les articles & les noms** *11*

CHAPITRE 4 : **Les adjectifs** *16*

CHAPITRE 5 : **La forme interrogative** *21*

CHAPITRE 6 : **La forme négative** *26*

CHAPITRE 7 : **Les pronoms directs & indirects** *31*

CHAPITRE 8 : **Les pronoms EN & Y** *36*

CHAPITRE 9 : **Les adjectifs possessifs** *40*

CHAPITRE 10 : **Les adjectifs démonstratifs** *45*

CHAPITRE 11 : **Les verbes pronominaux** *50*

CHAPITRE 12 : **Les comparatifs** *55*

CHAPITRE 13 : **Les superlatifs** *60*

CHAPITRE 14 : **Le présent** *65*

CHAPITRE 15 : **L'impératif** *70*

CHAPITRE 16 : **Le passé composé** *74*

CHAPITRE 17 : **L'imparfait** *78*

CHAPITRE 18 : **Le futur proche & le futur simple** *82*

CHAPITRE 19 : **Le conditionnel** *86*

CHAPITRE 20 : **Test diagnostique** *90*

INTRODUCTION

Test d'évaluation

Choisissez la bonne réponse :

1/ Achetez-vous <u>une nouvelle voiture</u> ? Oui, j' _____.
  a/ l'achète
  b/ en achète
  c/ y achète
  d/ en achète une

2/ Hier, elles _____ dans la forêt.
  a/ sont sortis
  b/ sont sorties
  c/ ont sorti
  d/ va sortir

3/ _____ étudiante habite dans _____ appartement.
  a/ Cet/cette
  b/ Cette/cet
  c/ Cette/cette
  d/ Cet/cet

4/ Je _____ ce poème.
  a/ comprend
  b/ compris
  c/ comprenne
  d/ comprends

5/ _____ tablette et _____ ordinateur sur son bureau.
  a/ Ma/mon
  b/ Mon/ma
  c/ Mon/mon
  d/ Ma/ma

6/ Les _____ dans ce musée sont _____.

a/ tableau/beau
b/ tableaux/belles
c/ tableaux/beaux
d/ tableaux/beau

7/ Il va _____ lycée tous les jours.

a/ à la
b/ au
c/ en
d/ dans le

8/ _____ jouez-vous au ping-pong ? Chez mon oncle.

a/ Où
b/ Quand
c/ Pourquoi
d/ Comment

9/ La pizza aux quatre fromages est _____.

a/ le mieux
b/ la meilleure
c/ le meilleur
d/ mieux

10/ Études-tu toujours l'italien ? Non, je _____ l'italien.

a/ n'étudie pas
b/ ne pas étudier
c/ n'étudie
d/ n'étudie plus

11/ Si tu avais rendez-vous, tu _____ un médecin plus tôt.

a/ voyais
b/ a vu
c/ voyait
d/ verrais

12/ La maison de Sarah est _____ et _____.

a/ vieille/poussiéreux
b/ vieil/poussiéreuse
c/ vieille/poussiéreuse
d/ vieux/ poussiéreuse

13/ Tu _____ boire un café si tu_____.

a/ peux/veux
b/ peut/veux
c/ peut/veux
d/ peut/veut

14/ Vous _____ faim et vous _____ très fatiguée.

a/ êtes/avez
b/ avez/avez
c/ avez/êtes
d/ êtes/êtes

15/ Elle a _____ et elle a _____ ce roman en français.

a/ lue/comprise
b/ lu/compris
c/ lu/comprise
d/ lue/compris

16/ Nous _____ à six heures du matin.

a/ se lever
b/ nous levons
c/ vous levez
d/ levons

17/ _____ allez-vous travailler ? Dans une heure.

a/ Où
b/ Quoi
c/ Comment
d/ Quand

18/ Pierre _____ quand son frère est arrivé.

a/ mange
b/ a mangé
c/ mangeait
d/ mangeais

19/ Allez-vous _____ club de gym ? Oui, j'_____ vais

a/ au/y
b/ au/en
c/ à/y
d/ en/y

20/ Il boit _____ eau mais ne boit pas _____ café.

a/ de l'/du
b/ du/du
c/ de l'/de
d/ de/du

21/ _____ un avocat et _____ excellent.

a/ Il est/c'est
b/ C'est/il est
c/ Il est/il est
d/ C'est/c'est

22/ _____ fille est petite et _____ fils est grand.

a/ Sa/sa
b/ Son/son
c/ Son/sa
d/ Sa/son

23/ _____ un sandwich, s'il te plaît.

a/ Donnes
b/ Donne-moi
c/ Donnes-en
d/ Me donner

24/ Elle parle _____ français que sa cousine.

a/ meilleure
b/ meilleur
c/ mieux
d/ le mieux

25/ Je _____ me reposer et ils _____ étudier.

a/ dois/doivent
b/ doit/doivent
c/ dois/doive
d/ doit/doivent

RÉPONSES:

1/d	6/c	11/d	16/b	21/b
2/b	7/b	12/c	17/d	22/d
3/b	8/a	13/a	18/c	23/b
4/d	9/b	14/c	19/a	24/c
5/a	10/d	15/b	20/c	25/a

SCORE : _____ /25

NOTES :

CHAPITRE 1

Les verbes au présent : être, avoir, aller, pouvoir, vouloir

Choisissez la bonne réponse :

1/ Je _____ français.

   a/ sont
   b/ suis
   c/ es
   d/ est

2/ Elle _____ manger.

   a/ veut
   b/ veux
   c/ veulent
   d/ voulons

3/ Sophie et moi _____ au cinéma.

   a/ vont
   b/ allez
   c/ allons
   d/ vais

4/ Mes parents _____ deux voitures.

   a/ avons
   b/ ai
   c/ a
   d/ ont

5/ Vous _____ acheter un livre.

   a/ peut
   b/ pouvez
   c/ peux
   d/ peuvent

6/ Je _____ à la bibliothèque.

    a/ vas

    b/ allez

    c/ va

    d/ vais

7/ Vous _____ fatigué.

    a/ sommes

    b/ êtes

    c/ suis

    d/ sont

8/ Nous _____ voyager.

    a/ voulons

    b/ veux

    c/ veulent

    d/ veut

9/ Tu _____ dormir.

    a/ vais

    b/ vont

    c/ allez

    d/ vas

10/ Nous _____ une maison.

    a/ avez

    b/ avons

    c/ ont

    d/ ai

11/ Elle _____ jouer au tennis.

    a/ peux

    b/ peuvent

    c/ peut

    d/ pouvez

12/ Ils _____ Américains.

a/ sommes
b/ sont
c/ suis
d/ est

13/ Ils _____ à Bordeaux.

a/ va
b/ vont
c/ va
d/ vais

14/ Tu _____ venir à Paris ?

a/ veut
b/ voulez
c/ veux
d/ veut

15/ Vous _____ des amis.

a/ a
b/ avez
c/ avons
d/ ont

16/ Vous _____ regarder un film.

a/ allons
b/ allez
c/ vas
d/ vais

17/ Tu _____ jeune.

a/ est
b/ sommes
c/ es
d/ suis

18/ J(e) _____ un frère.

   a/ 'ai
   b/ as
   c/ avez
   d/ ont

19/ Tu _____ travailler.

   a/ peux
   b/ peut
   c/ pouvons
   d/ peuvent

20/ Elles _____ danser.

   a/ voulons
   b/ veut
   c/ veulent
   d/ veux

21/ Elle _____ téléphoner.

   a/ va
   b/ vas
   c/ vais
   d/ vont

22/ Elle _____ une moto rouge.

   a/ as
   b/ ai
   c/ a
   d/ avez

23/ Nous _____ faire du ski.

   a/ pouvez
   b/ pouvons
   c/ peut
   d/ peux

24/ Nous _____ contents.

    a/ est
    b/ es
    c/ sont
    d/ sommes

25/ Je _____ lire un magazine.

    a/ veut
    b/ veulent
    c/ veux
    d/ voulons

RÉPONSES :

1/b	6/d	11/c	16/b	21/a
2/a	7/b	12/b	17/c	22/c
3/c	8/a	13/b	18/a	23/b
4/d	9/d	14/c	19/a	24/d
5/b	10/b	15/b	20/c	25/c

SCORE : _____/25

NOTES :

CHAPITRE 2

C'est, Il/Elle est, Il y a (les prépositions)

Choisissez la bonne réponse :

1/ _____ un étudiant anglais.
  a/ Il est
  b/ C'est
  c/ Il peut
  d/ Ce sont

2/ Nous allons _____ la boulangerie.
  a/ de
  b/ pour
  c/ à
  d/ par

3/ _____ allemande.
  a/ C'est
  b/ C'est un
  c/ Elle est
  d/ Il est

4/ _____ un chien dans la rue.
  a/ Elle est
  b/ Il est
  c/ Il y a
  d/ Il est

5/ Le chat est _____ la table.
  a/ à
  b/ par
  c/ de
  d/ sous

6/ _____ médecin.

    a/ Il est
    b/ C'est
    c/ Il y a
    d/ Elle est un

7/ _____ mon meilleur ami.

    a/ Il
    b/ Il est
    c/ C'est
    d/ Il y a

8/ _____ des stylos sur le bureau.

    a/ Il y a
    b/ Ces
    c/ C'est
    d/ Ils sont

9/ Le vélo est _____ le balcon.

    a/ pour
    b/ à
    c/ par
    d/ sur

10/ _____ des professeurs.

    a/ Ils sont
    b/ Ce sont
    c/ C'est
    d/ Il est

11/ _____ un très beau village à visiter.

    a/ Elle est
    b/ Ce
    c/ Il est
    d/ Il y a

12/ Le chat de Paul ? _____ est adorable.

    a/ C'est
    b/ Elle est
    c/ Il est
    d/ Il y a

13/ _____ vraiment joli ici !

    a/ Il y a
    b/ C'est un
    c/ Elle est
    d/ C'est

14/ _____ petites.

    a/ Ils sont
    b/ Elles sont
    c/ Il est
    d/ Elle est

15/ _____ une pomme dans le panier.

    a/ Il y a
    b/ Il est
    c/ Elle est
    d/ Elles sont

16/ J'achète un cadeau _____ ma mère.

    a/ par
    b/ de
    c/ pour
    d/ sur

17/ _____ des journalistes.

    a/ C'est
    b/ Ce sont
    c/ Il est
    d/ Ils sont

18/ _____ intelligentes et éduquées.

    a/ C'est
    b/ Elles sont
    c/ Ils sont
    d/ Ce sont

19/ _____ des portables dans le sac.

    a/ C'est
    b/ Ils sont
    c/ Il y a
    d/ Il est

20/ Elle parle _____ son père.

    a/ sur
    b/ par
    c/ sous
    d/ à

21/ _____ un avion indien.

    a/ Elle est
    b/ Il est
    c/ C'est
    d/ Ce sont

22/ _____ malades.

    a/ Elle est
    b/ Elles sont
    c/ Il est
    d/ Il y a

23/ _____ plusieurs ordinateurs.

    a/ Il y a
    b/ Elle est
    c/ Il est
    d/ C'est

24/ La mère est assise _____ son fils.

    a/ pour
    b/ par
    c/ à côté de
    d/ à

25/ Nous venons _____ Normandie.

    a/ de
    b/ par
    c/ pour
    d/ derrière

RÉPONSES :

1/b	6/a	11/d	16/c	21/c
2/c	7/c	12/c	17/b	22/b
3/c	8/a	13/d	18/b	23/a
4/c	9/d	14/b	19/c	24/c
5/d	10/b	15/a	20/d	25/a

SCORE : _____ /25

NOTES :

CHAPITRE 3

Les articles & les noms

Choisissez la bonne réponse :

1/ _____ veste et _____ pantalon.
    a/ La/la
    b/ Le/la
    c/ La/le
    d/ Le/le

2/ _____ tables et _____ chaise.
    a/ La/la
    b/ Les/la
    c/ Les/le
    d/ Les/les

3/ Les _____ et les _____ .
    a/ manteau/chaussures
    b/ manteaux/chaussure
    c/ manteaux/chaussures
    d/ manteau/chaussure

4/ _____ pizza et _____ gâteau.
    a/ La/le
    b/ Le/la
    c/ L'/l
    d/ L/l'

5/ _____ jeune homme et _____ jeune femme.
    a/ La/le
    b/ Le/la
    c/ L'/l'
    d/ La/l'

6/ _____ étudiante et _____ artiste.

   a/ L'/le
   b/ La/l'
   c/ L'/le
   d/ L'/l'

7/ _____ café et _____ eau.

   a/ Le/la
   b/ La/le
   c/ Le/l'
   d/ La/la

8/ Les _____ et _____ télévision.

   a/ bureau/la
   b/ bureaux/la
   c/ bureaux/l'
   d/ bureaux/les

9/ Audrey est grand-mère. Elle a trois _____ et deux _____.

   a/ petites filles/petits-fils
   b/ petites-filles/petits-fils
   c/ petites filles/petits-fils
   d/ petite-fille/petits fils

10/ Deux _____ et trois _____.

   a/ oiseau/animaux
   b/ oiseaux/animal
   c/ oiseaux/animaux
   d/ oiseau/animal

11/ Il est _____ et elle est _____.

   a/ infirmier/médecine
   b/ infirmière/médecin
   c/ infirmière/médecine
   d/ infirmier/médecin

12/ Le pluriel de « œil » est _____.

a/ œufs
b/ vœux
c/ yeux
d/ eux

13/ _____ hôtel et _____ appartement.

a/ L'/le
b/ Le/l'
c/ La/l'
d/ L'/l'

14/ _____ enfants et _____ parents.

a/ L'/les
b/ Les/les
c/ Les/l'
d/ La/les

15/ Elle boit _____ thé mais ne boit pas _____ vin.

a/ du/de
b/ de/de
c/ d'/du
d/ de/le

16/ La _____ et la_____.

a/ directrice/vendeuses
b/ directrice/vendeuse
c/ directeur/vendeur
d/ directrices/vendeuse

17/ Robert est _____et Chantal est_____.

a/ candidat/examinatrice
b/ candidate/examinateur
c/ candidat/examinateur
d/ candidate/examinateur

18/ Elle achète des _____ et des _____.

    a/ journal/couteau
    b/ journaux/couteau
    c/ journal/couteaux
    d/ journaux/couteaux

19/ Marc est _____. Valérie est _____.

    a/ boulanger/boulangère
    b/ boulangère/boulanger
    c/ boulangerie/boulangère
    d/ boulangère/boulangère

20/ La _____de ma mère est ma _____.

    a/ belle-fille/cousin
    b/ grand-mère/nièce
    c/ sœur/grand-mère
    d/ sœur/tante

21/ Le fils de mon frère est mon _____

    a/ cousin
    b/ neveu
    c/ nerveux
    d/ gendre

22/ _____ chemise est _____ et _____.

    a/ La/blanche/sèche
    b/ Le/blanc/sec
    c/ Le/blanche/sèche
    d/ La/blanche/sec

23/ La _____ est _____.

    a/ prince/musicien
    b/ princesse/musicienne
    c/ princesse/musicien
    d/ prince/musicienne

24/ La _____ est _____ du monde.

a/ nageur/champion
b/ nageuse/champion
c/ nageuse/championne
d/ natation/championne

25/ Ma _____ est _____ dans cette université.

a/ cousine/employé
b/ cousine/employée
c/ cousin/employé
d/ cousins/employée

RÉPONSES:

1/c	6/d	11/d	16/b	21/b
2/b	7/c	12/c	17/a	22/a
3/c	8/b	13/d	18/d	23/b
4/a	9/b	14/b	19/a	24/c
5/b	10/c	15/a	20/d	25/b

SCORE : _____ **/25**

NOTES :

CHAPITRE 4

Les adjectifs

Choisissez la bonne réponse :

1/ Ana est _____ et Carolina est _____.
   a/ brésilien/américain
   b/ brésilien/américaine
   c/ brésilienne/américain
   d/ brésilienne/américaine

2/ Marie est _____ de ses enfants.
   a/ fier
   b/ fière
   c/ fières
   d/ fiers

3/ La veste est _____ et _____.
   a/ gris/démodée
   b/ grise/démodé
   c/ gris/démodée
   d/ grise/ démodée

4/ Les étudiants sont _____ et les étudiantes sont _____.
   a/ content/ravis
   b/ contentes/ravies
   c/ contents/ravie
   d/ contents/ravies

5/ Marcel est _____ et Marianne est _____.
   a/ veuf/veuve
   b/ veuve/veuf
   c/ veuve/veuve
   d/ veuf/veuf

6/ Les pantalons sont _____ et les chaussettes sont _____.

a/ vert/marron
b/ vertes/marrons
c/ verts/marron
d/ verts/marrons

7/ Les pommes sont _____ et _____.

a/ grosse/rouge
b/ grosses/rouges
c/ gros/rouge
d/ gros/rouges

8/ Rachida est _____ et Paul est _____.

a/ gentil/paresseux
b/ gentille/paresseuse
c/ gentil/paresseuse
d/ gentille/paresseux

9/ La robe est _____ et _____.

a/ belle/élégant
b/ beau/élégant
c/ belle/élégante
d/ belles/élégant

10/ Les fraises sont _____ et _____.

a/ bons/sucrés
b/ bonnes/sucrées
c/ bons/sucrées
d/ bonnes/sucrés

11/ Marie est _____ et _____.

a/ active/sportif
b/ actif/sportif
c/ active/sportive
d/ activée/sportive

12/ _____ voiture est _____.

   a/ Le/vieille

   b/ La/vieux

   c/ Le/vieux

   d/ La/vieille

13/ _____ soupe est _____.

   a/ La/froide

   b/ La/froid

   c/ Le/froid

   d/ Le/froide

14/ _____ fiancée est _____.

   a/ La/heureux

   b/ Le/heureuse

   c/ La/heureuse

   d/ Le/heureux

15/ Cette histoire est _____ et _____.

   a/ ancien/cruel

   b/ ancienne/cruel

   c/ ancien/cruelle

   d/ ancienne/cruelle

16/ Elle est _____ et _____

   a/ travailleuse/motivée

   b/ travailleur/motivé

   c/ travailleuse/motivé

   d/ travail/motivée

17/ L'ouvrier est _____ et _____.

   a/ courageuse/patiente

   b/ courageux/patiente

   c/ courage/patience

   d/ courageux/patient

18/ Ces légendes sont _____ et _____.

    a/ intéressants/passionnantes
    b/ intéressantes/passionnantes
    c/ intéressantes/passionnants
    d/ intéressante/passionnantes

19/ Cette baguette est _____ et _____.

    a/ légère/croustillant
    b/ léger/croustillant
    c/ léger/croustillante
    d/ légère/croustillante

20/ L'exposition Picasso est _____ et _____.

    a/ merveilleuse/sensationnelle
    b/ merveilleux/sensationnelle
    c/ merveilleuse/sensationnel
    d/ merveilleux/sensationnel

21/ Il est _____ et elle _____.

    a/ danseuse/actrice
    b/ danseur/acteur
    c/ danseur/actrice
    d/ danseurs/actrice

22/ Luis est _____ et Maria est _____.

    a/ mexicain/ norvégienne
    b/ mexicaine/ norvégienne
    c/ mexicain/norvégien
    d/ mexicaine/ norvégien

23/ Il achète des casquettes _____ pour ses amis.

    a/ australien
    b/ australiennes
    c/ australienne
    d/ australiens

24/ C'est une étudiante _____ et _____.

   a/ consciencieux/ambitieuse
   b/ consciencieuse/ambitieux
   c/ consciencieux/ambitieuses
   d/ consciencieuse/ambitieuse

25/ Il y a de _____ chambres _____ dans cette maison.

   a/ belles/décorées
   b/ beaux/décorés
   c/ belles/décorés
   d/ beaux/décorées

RÉPONSES:

1/d	6/c	11/c	16/a	21/c
2/b	7/b	12/d	17/d	22/a
3/d	8/d	13/a	18/b	23/b
4/d	9/c	14/c	19/d	24/d
5/a	10/b	15/d	20/a	25/a

SCORE : _____ /25

NOTES :

CHAPITRE 5

La forme interrogative

Choisissez la bonne réponse :

1/ _____ fais-tu ?

    a/ Où
    b/ Quand
    c/ Qu'est-ce que
    d/ Que

2/ _____ habites-tu ? J'habite à Paris.

    a/ Quand
    b/ Où
    c/ Quoi
    d/ Qu'est-ce que

3/ _____ es-tu née ? En 1976.

    a/ Pourquoi
    b/ À quoi
    c/ Où
    d/ Quand

4/ _____ le chien est gentil ?

    a/ Quoi
    b/ Que
    c/ Qu'est-ce que
    d/ Est-ce que

5/ _____ heure est-il ?

    a/ Quel
    b/ Quoi
    c/ Quelle
    d/ Que

6/ _____ toujours un croissant le matin ?

a/ Que manges-tu
b/ Manges-tu
c/ Qu'est-ce que tu manges
d/ Mange

7/ Entre ces deux chemises, _____ préfères-tu ?

a/ Laquelle
b/ Quelle
c/ Duquel
d/ Quoi

8/ _____ as-tu besoin ? J'ai besoin d'une voiture.

a/ À quoi
b/ De quoi
c/ Pourquoi
d/ Sur quoi

9/ _____ vas-tu te coucher ? Parce que j'ai sommeil.

a/ Pourquoi
b/ Où
c/ A quoi
d/ De quoi

10/ _____ études voulez-vous faire ?

a/ Laquelle
b/ Quels
c/ Quelle
d/ Quelles

11/ _____ ordinateur veux-tu acheter ?

a/ Quels
b/ Quelles
c/ Quel
d/ Que

12/ _____bois-tu du thé chaud ? Parce que j'ai froid.

a/ Quoi
b/ Pourquoi
c/ De quoi
d/ À quoi

13/ _____habitez-vous aux États-Unis ? Trois ans.

a/ Depuis quand
b/ Depuis
c/ Quand
d/ Pour quand

14/ _____ le chien dans le jardin ?

a/ Que vois-tu
b/ Qu'est-ce que tu vois
c/ Quoi
d/ Vois-tu

15/ _____ joue-t-il au tennis ? Il joue très bien.

a/ Que
b/ Pourquoi
c/ Quoi
d/ Comment

16/ _____ est venu hier soir ?

a/ Qui
b/ Quoi
c/ Quand
d/ À qui

17/ _____ frères as-tu ?

a/ Combien
b/ Combien de
c/ Qui
d/ À qui

18/ _____ il comprend ce texte en anglais ?

a/ Quoi
b/ Comprend-il
c/ Est-ce qu'
d/ Est-ce que

19/ _____ sont tes animaux préférés ?

a/ Quels
b/ Quelles
c/ Quel
d/ Quelle

20/ _____ heure finit le cours de français ?

a/ À quel
b/ Quand
c/ Où
d/ À quelle

21/ _____ va-t-elle voyager ? Avec ses parents.

a/ Comment
b/ Pourquoi
c/ Avec qui
d/ Quoi

22/ _____ allez-vous faire du camping ? Dans une semaine.

a/ Pourquoi
b/ Combien
c/ Comment
d/ Quand

23/ _____ étudies-tu ? Les mathématiques.

a/ Qu'est-ce que
b/ Pourquoi
c/ Qu'
d/ Que

24/ _____ Rebecca travaille-t-elle ? Dans un restaurant.

a/ Quand
b/ Combien
c/ Quand
d/ Où

25/ Entre ces deux manteaux, _____ veux-tu mettre ?

a/ laquelle
b/ lequel
c/ lesquelles
d/ lesquels

RÉPONSES :

1/d	6/b	11/c	16/a	21/c
2/b	7/a	12/b	17/b	22/d
3/d	8/b	13/a	18/c	23/c
4/d	9/a	14/d	19/a	24/d
5/c	10/d	15/d	20/d	25/b

SCORE : _____ /25

NOTES :

CHAPITRE 6

La forme négative

Choisissez la bonne réponse :

1/ Est-elle française ? Non, _____ française.
 a/ elle n'est pas
 b/ elle n'est
 c/ elle est
 d/ ne pas

2/ Étudies-tu l'espagnol ? Non, je _____ l'espagnol.
 a/ n'étudie
 b/ étudie pas
 c/ n'étudie pas
 d/ ne pas étudier

3/ Connais-tu quelqu'un ici ? Non, je _____.
 a/ ne connais rien
 b/ ne connais pas
 c/ ne connais personne
 d/ ne pas connaître

4/ Manges-tu toujours de la viande ? Non, je _____.
 a/ ne mange plus de viande.
 b/ ne mange pas de viande.
 c/ ne mange pas encore de viande.
 d/ ne mange rien.

5/ Ont-ils regardé la télé ? Non, ils _____ la télé.
 a/ ne sont pas regardés
 b/ ne regardent pas
 c/ ne pas regarder
 d/ n'ont pas regardé

6/ Savez-vous si Michel fait ses devoirs ? Non, je _____.

a/ sais pas
b/ ne sais pas
c/ ne sais plus
d/ ne sais pas encore

7/ Font-ils du ski ? Non, ils _____ ski.

a/ ne font pas de
b/ ne font pas
c/ ne fait pas de
d/ ne font pas du

8/ Voulez-vous quelque chose ? Non, je _____.

a/ ne veux personne
b/ ne veux rien
c/ ne veut pas
d/ rien

9/ Allez-vous faire la cuisine ? Non, nous _____ faire la cuisine.

a/ ne pas aller
b/ n'allons pas
c/ n'allez pas
d/ pas

10/ Aimes-tu les épinards ? Non, je _____ les épinards.

a/ n'aime
b/ n'aime
c/ rien
d/ n'aime pas

11/ Avez-vous quelque chose à manger ? Non, nous _____ à manger.

a/ n'avons rien
b/ n'avons personne
c/ n'avons plus
d/ n'avons pas encore

12/ Voyagez-vous samedi ? Non, je _____ ce jour-là.

a/ ne voyage
b/ ne voyage pas
c/ voyage pas
d/ ne pas voyager

13/ Simon écoute-t-il encore du rap ? Non, il _____.

a/ n'écoute pas de rap
b/ pas encore écouter de rap
c/ ne pas écouter de rap
d/ n'écoute plus de rap

14/ Est-ce que vous faites une fête ? Non, nous_____ de fête.

a/ ne faites pas
b/ ne faisons
c/ ne faisons pas
d/ ne fait jamais

15/ Comprends-tu quelque chose à ce film ? Non, je_____.

a/ n'y comprends rien
b/ comprend peu
c/ comprends
d/ comprend rien

16/ Fais-tu souvent du vélo ? Non, je_____.

a/ fais pas du vélo
b/ ne fais jamais de vélo
c/ fais pas de vélo
d/ ne fais rien

17/ Peux-tu me prêter 50 euros ? Non, je _____.

a/ ne peux rien
b/ ne peux
c/ ne peux pas
d/ ne peux rien

18/ A-t-elle un chat ? Non, elle _____ chat.

a/ n'a pas un
b/ n'a pas de
c/ n'a pas deux
d/ n'a personne

19/ Est-ce que vous attendez quelqu'un ? Non, _____.

a/ rien
b/ ne pas
c/ personne
d/ ne pas encore

20/ Jette le lait. Il _____.

a/ n'est plus bon
b/ est pas bon
c/ n'est pas encore bon
d/ pas toujours bon

21/ _____ ce film d'horreur ! Il fait trop peur.

a/ Ne pas regarder
b/ Ne regarde pas
c/ Regarde pas
d/ Ne regarde rien

22/ Est-ce qu'il vient parfois à la campagne ? Non, il _____.

a/ ne viens jamais
b/ vient jamais
c/ ne vient jamais
d/ ne viennent jamais

23/ Est-ce que vous allez quelque part ? Non, je _____.

a/ ne vais pas
b/ ne vais nulle part
c/ ne vas nulle part
d/ ne vais pas encore

24/ Achetez-vous des gants ? Non, nous _____.

    a/ n'achetons pas de gants
    b/ n'achetons pas les gants
    c/ n'achetons plus des gants
    d/ achetons des gants

25/ Aimes-tu les orchidées ? Non, je _____ orchidées.

    a/ n'aime pas des
    b/ n'aime pas encore
    c/ n'aime rien
    d/ n'aime pas les

RÉPONSES :

1/a	6/b	11/a	16/b	21/b
2/c	7/a	12/b	17/c	22/c
3/c	8/b	13/d	18/b	23/b
4/a	9/b	14/c	19/c	24/a
5/d	10/d	15/a	20/a	25/d

SCORE : _____/25

NOTES :

CHAPITRE 7

Les pronoms directs & indirects

Choisissez la bonne réponse :

1/ Lis-tu <u>le livre</u> ? Oui, je _____lis.

a/ le
b/ la
c/ lui
d/ leur

2/ Parlez-vous <u>à vos amis</u> ? Oui, nous _____parlons.

a/ la
b/ les
c/ leur
d/ lui

3/ Donnes-tu <u>les fruits aux enfants</u> ? Oui, je _____ donne.

a/ les lui
b/ les leur
c/ le leur
d/ lui leur

4/ Est-ce qu'elle parle <u>à sa tante</u> ? Oui, elle _____ parle.

a/ leur
b/ vous
c/ nous
d/ lui

5/ Voulez-vous acheter <u>ces guitares</u> ? Oui, je _____.

a/ veux les acheter
b/ veux acheter
c/ veut lui acheter
d/ veux leur acheter

6/ Peux-tu <u>m'aider</u> ? <u>Oui, je</u> peux _____.

    a/ aider

    b/ t'aider

    c/ l'aider

    d/ s'aider

7/ Regardes-tu <u>le match de tennis</u> ? Oui, je _____.

    a/ la regarde

    b/ le regardes

    c/ les regarde

    d/ le regarde

8/ Visitez-vous <u>les appartements</u> ? Oui, nous _____.

    a/ les visitons

    b/ les visites

    c/ les visitez

    d/ le visitez

9/ Est-ce que vous louez <u>la maison</u> ? Oui, nous _____.

    a/ le louons

    b/ les louons

    c/ la louons

    d/ en louons

10/ Achetez-vous des livres <u>à Karine</u> ? Oui, je _____ des livres.

    a/ lui acheter

    b/ leur achète

    c/ lui achète

    d/ les achète

11/ Est-ce que ta copine <u>t'envoie</u> <u>ton cadeau</u> ? Oui, elle _____.

    a/ me les envoie

    b/ te l'envoie

    c/ leur envoie

    d/ me l'envoie

12/ Vas-tu faire le lit ? Oui, je _____.

a/ vais leur faire
b/ vais la faire
c/ vais le faire
d/ vais faire

13/ Collectionnez-vous les montres ? Oui, je _____.

a/ les collectionne
b/ les collectionnes
c/ la collectionne
d/ les collectionnent

14/ Explique la leçon à Julie. Explique- _____.

a/ les-lui
b/ le-lui
c/ la-lui
d/ la leur

15/ Veux-tu conduire la voiture ? Non, _____.

a/ conduis-le
b/ conduis-la
c/ conduisez là
d/ conduisons-la

16/ Est-ce vous pouvez nous attendre ? Oui, nous _____.

a/ pouvons attendre
b/ pouvons l'attendre
c/ pouvons vous attendre
d/ pouvons les attendre

17/ Répondent-ils au président ? Oui, ils _____

a/ vous répondent
b/ leur répondent
c/ me répondent
d/ lui répondent

18/ Allez-vous laver <u>la cuisine</u> ? Oui, je _____.

a/ vais laver
b/ vais les laver
c/ vais laver là
d/ vais la laver

19/ Est-ce que tu as construit <u>cette maison</u> ? Oui, je _____.

a/ l'ai construite
b/ l'ai construit
c/ la construit
d/ le construit

20/ Jeanne et Claire ? _____ à dîner samedi soir ?

a/ Vous invitez
b/ Tu l'invites
c/ Les invites-tu
d/ L'invites-tu

21/ Manges-tu <u>les fruits</u> ? Oui, je _____ mange.

a/ le
b/ les
c/ l'
d/ leur

22/ Peux-tu couper <u>cette tranche de pain</u> ? Oui, je _____ couper.

a/ peux la
b/ peux le
c/ peut la
d/ peux lui

23/ Aimez-vous <u>les desserts</u> ? Non, je _____.

a/ ne l'aime pas
b/ ne les aimes pas
c/ ne pas l'aimer
d/ ne les aime pas

24/ Avez-vous entendu <u>la réponse</u> ? Oui, nous _____.

    a/ l'avons entendu
    b/ l'avons entendue
    c/ les avons entendus
    d/ avons entendu

25/ Écris-tu à <u>tes parents</u> ? Oui, je _____ chaque semaine.

    a/ leur écrit
    b/ leur écris
    c/ lui écris
    d/ lui écrit

RÉPONSES :

1/a	6/b	11/d	16/c	21/b
2/c	7/d	12/c	17/d	22/a
3/b	8/a	13/a	18/d	23/d
4/d	9/c	14/c	19/a	24/b
5/a	10/c	15/b	20/c	25/b

SCORE : _____ **/25**

NOTES :

CHAPITRE 8

Les pronoms EN & Y

Choisissez la bonne réponse :

1/ Est-ce que vous buvez <u>du thé</u> ? Oui, nous _____ buvons.
  a/ en
  b/ y

2/ Ils vont <u>au cinéma</u>. Ils _____ vont.
  a/ y
  b/ en

3/ Elle pense <u>au film</u>. Elle _____ pense.
  a/ en
  b/ y

4/ Vous achetez <u>des gants</u>. Vous _____ achetez.
  a/ en
  b/ y

5/ Elles jouent <u>au poker</u>. Elles _____ jouent.
  a/ en
  b/ y

6/ Est-ce que tu vas <u>à la piscine</u> ? Oui, j'_____vais.
  a/ en
  b/ y

7/ Il répare <u>des ordinateurs.</u> Il _____ répare beaucoup.
  a/ y
  b/ en

8/ Veux-tu préparer <u>une omelette</u> ? Oui, je _____.

    a/ veux en préparer une

    b/ veux en préparer

9/ Est-ce que je peux aller <u>à la fête</u> ? Oui, Vas-_____.

    a/ y

    b/ en

10/ Tu manges <u>des fruits</u> ? Oui, j'_____ mange.

    a/ en

    b/ y

11/ Habites-tu <u>dans cette maison</u> ? Oui, j'_____habite.

    a/ en

    b/ y

12/ Réfléchis-tu <u>à notre projet</u> ? Oui, j'_____ réfléchis.

    a/ en

    b/ y

13/ Est-ce qu'elle fait <u>du sport</u> <u>au club</u> ? Oui, elle _____ fait.

    a/ y en

    b/ en y

14/ Tu regardes <u>des photos</u> ? Oui, j'_____ regarde.

    a/ en

    b/ y

15/ Voulez-vous voyager <u>en France</u> ? Oui, nous_____ voyager.

    a/ voulons y

    b/ voulons en

16/ Les plantes sont-elles <u>dans le jardin</u> ? Oui, elles _____ sont.

    a/ y

    b/ en

17/ A-t-elle a adopté <u>un chiot</u> ? Non, elle _____a adopté trois.

a/ y
b/ en

18/ Voulez-vous <u>un jus de fruits</u> ? Oui, j'_____.

a/ en veux
b/ en veux un

19/ Mon portefeuille est-il <u>dans la voiture</u> ? Oui, il _____ est.

a/ y
b/ en

20/ Est-ce que tu profites <u>de tes vacances</u> ? Oui, j'_____ profite.

a/ en
b/ y

21/ Travaillez-vous <u>dans ce bureau</u> ? Oui, j'_____ travaille.

a/ en
b/ y

22/ Elle a aimé ses vacances <u>en Grèce</u>. Elle veut_____ retourner.

a/ y
b/ en

23/ <u>De la salade de tomates</u>, vous _____ voulez ?

a/ y
b/ en

24/ Le bébé dort-il <u>sur le sofa</u> ? Oui, il _____ dort.

a/ en
b/ y

25/ Commandes-tu <u>une pizza</u> ? Oui, j'_____ commande une.

a/ en
b/ y

RÉPONSES :

1/a	6/b	11/b	16/a	21/b
2/a	7/b	12/b	17/b	22/a
3/b	8/a	13/a	18/b	23/b
4/a	9/a	14/a	19/a	24/b
5/b	10/a	15/a	20/a	25/a

SCORE : _____ /25

NOTES :

CHAPITRE 9

Les adjectifs possessifs

Choisissez la bonne réponse :

1/ Voici _____ mère et _____ père.

    a/ mon/ma
    b/ ma/ma
    c/ ma/mon
    d/ mon/mon

2/ Il monte dans _____ voiture.

    a/ son
    b/ sa
    c/ ses
    d/ se

3/ Vous voyagez avec _____ amis.

    a/ son
    b/ ma
    c/ sa
    d/ vos

4/ _____ parents vont l'accompagner à la gare.

    a/ Ses
    b/ Son
    c/ Sa
    d/ Se

5/ Tu fais _____ devoirs après l'école.

    a/ ton
    b/ son
    c/ tes
    d/ sa

6/ _____ ordinateur ne fonctionne plus.

a/ Sa
b/ Son
c/ Ses
d/ Sont

7/ Enlève _____ chaussures. Elles sont sales.

a/ ton
b/ ta
c/ tes
d/ t'es

8/ Ils invitent _____ amis à passer un weekend chez eux.

a/ leur
b/ son
c/ leurs
d/ l'heure

9/ Nous avons _____ bureau dans cet immeuble.

a/ notre
b/ nous
c/ nos
d/ le nôtre

10/ Donne-moi _____ avis sur cette situation.

a/ ta
b/ ton
c/ sa
d/ tu

11/ J'aime beaucoup _____ style vestimentaire.

a/ leur
b/ la
c/ lui
d/ sont

12/ _____ valises sont trop lourdes.

a/ ma
b/ mes
c/ mon
d/ me

13/ _____ chambre est prête, Madame.

a/ Vous
b/ La vôtre
c/ Vos
d/ Votre

14/ _____ chien ne veut pas sortir dans la rue.

a/ Sa
b/ Ses
c/ Se
d/ Son

15/ Les bougies sur _____ gâteau sont très petites.

a/ mon
b/ ma
c/ me
d/ sa

16/ N'oublie pas de prendre _____ sac à dos pour le voyage.

a/ votre
b/ sont
c/ ton
d/ ses

17/ _____ billets d'avion sont dans le tiroir.

a/ Tes
b/ Ton
c/ T'es
d/ Mon

18/ Est-ce que tu as pensé à _____ cadeau d'anniversaire ?

a/ leurs
b/ l'heure
c/ leur
d/ la

19/ Le chocolat chaud est _____ boisson préférée.

a/ nos
b/ nous
c/ notre
d/ le nôtre

20/ Ne touche pas à _____ collection de miniatures.

a/ sa
b/ son
c/ ses
d/ ça

21/ La décoration de _____ chambre est originale.

a/ votre
b/ vos
c/ vous
d/ la vôtre

22/ _____ raquette de tennis est cassée.

a/ Tu
b/ Ton
c/ Tes
d/ Ta

23/ La femme de _____ fils est ingénieure.

a/ sa
b/ sont
c/ son
d/ ce

24/ Ils organisent une réunion familiale pour _____ père.

    a/ ses
    b/ sa
    c/ mes
    d/ leur

25/ _____ portable est sur la table de la salle à manger.

    a/ Ma
    b/ Mon
    c/ Mes
    d/ Me

RÉPONSES :

1/c	6/b	11/a	16/c	21/a
2/b	7/c	12/b	17/a	22/d
3/d	8/c	13/d	18/c	23/c
4/a	9/a	14/d	19/c	24/d
5/c	10/b	15/a	20/a	25/b

SCORE : _____ /25

NOTES :

CHAPITRE 10

Les adjectifs démonstratifs

Choisissez la bonne réponse :

1/ _____acteur est très connu.
- a/ Ce
- b/ Cette
- c/ Cet
- d/ Ces

2/ Je veux acheter _____ rose pour ma mère.
- a/ ces
- b/ cette
- c/ cet
- d/ ce

3/ _____ voiture est trop vieille pour rouler.
- a/ Cet
- b/ Cette
- c/ Ce
- d/ Ces

4/ _____ lycée a une excellente réputation.
- a/ Ce
- b/ Cette
- c/ Cet
- d/ C'est

5/ Allons visiter _____ appartement.
- a/ ce
- b/ cette
- c/ ces
- d/ cet

6/ L'infirmière s'occupe de _____ enfants malades.

   a/ ce
   b/ ces
   c/ cet
   d/ cette

7/ _____ stylo n'écrit pas.

   a/ Cette
   b/ C'est
   c/ Ce
   d/ Cet

8/ _____ magazines sont très intéressants.

   a/ Ces
   b/ Cet
   c/ Ce
   d/ Cette

9/ Nous pouvons aller dîner dans _____ restaurant.

   a/ cet
   b/ ces
   c/ cette
   d/ ce

10/ _____ hôtel est situé près de l'océan.

   a/ Cette
   b/ Ces
   c/ Ce
   d/ Cet

11/ _____ glace au chocolat est délicieuse.

   a/ Cet
   b/ Ce
   c/ Cette
   d/ C'est

12/ _____ jeune homme s'appelle Steve.

   a/ Ce
   b/ Cet
   c/ Ces
   d/ C'est

13/ _____ journaux sont italiens.

   a/ Ce
   b/ Ces
   c/ Cet
   d/ Cette

14/ _____ activité me plaît beaucoup.

   a/ Ces
   b/ Cette
   c/ Cet
   d/ Ce

15/ Il faut changer _____ verre. Il est cassé.

   a/ cette
   b/ c'est
   c/ cet
   d/ ce

16/ _____ instruments de musique coûtent très cher.

   a/ Cette
   b/ Ce
   c/ Ces
   d/ C'est

17/ Ouvre _____ fenêtre, s'il te plaît.

   a/ cette
   b/ ces
   c/ cet
   d/ ce

18/ _____ jeunes filles suivent un cours de karaté.

a/ Ce
b/ Ses
c/ Ces
d/ C'est

19/ _____ tableau est italien.

a/ Ce
b/ Se
c/ Cet
d/ Cette

20/ _____ fourchette est sale. Ne l'utilise pas.

a/ Ces
b/ Cet
c/ Ces
d/ Cette

21/ Je veux acheter _____ ordinateur.

a/ cette
b/ cet
c/ ce
d/ ces

22/ _____ table ira dans la cuisine.

a/ Cette
b/ Cet
c/ C'est
d/ Ses

23/ _____ étudiant a gagné une bourse d'études.

a/ Cette
b/ Cet
c/ Ce
d/ C'est

24/ _____ professeurs font grève.

    a/ Ces
    b/ Ce
    c/ Cette
    d/ Cet

25/ _____ restaurant est le meilleur de la ville.

    a/ Ces
    b/ Cette
    c/ Ce
    d/ Cet

RÉPONSES :

1/c	6/b	11/c	16/c	21/b
2/b	7/c	12/a	17/a	22/a
3/b	8/a	13/b	18/c	23/b
4/a	9/d	14/b	19/a	24/a
5/d	10/d	15/d	20/d	25/c

SCORE : _____ /25

NOTES :

CHAPITRE 11

Les verbes pronominaux

Choisissez la bonne réponse

1/ Je _____ à huit heures le matin.
- a/ lève
- b/ me lève
- c/ me lever
- d/ lever

2/ Il _____ très rapidement.
- a/ réveille
- b/ a réveillé
- c/ réveiller
- d/ se réveille

3/ Nous _____ dans le parc pendant une heure.
- a/ promenons
- b/ nous promenons
- c/ se promènent
- d/ se promener

4/ Ils _____ à neuf heures du soir.
- a/ couchent
- b/ se couche
- c/ se coucher
- d/ se couchent

5/ Le contraire de « se réveiller » est :
- a/ se maquiller
- b/ se coucher
- c/ se lever
- d/ s'endormir

6/ Il faut _____ pour arriver à l'heure.

    a/ se dépêcher

    b/ dépêcher

    c/ dépêchons

    d/ dépêchera

7/ Ils _____ les mains plusieurs fois par jour.

    a/ se laver

    b/ se lave

    c/ se lavent

    d/ les lavent

8/ Le contraire de « parler » est

    a/ se taire

    b/ se disputer

    c/ se marier

    d/ s'intéresser à

9/ Vous _____ dents.

    a/ vous brossez les

    b/ vous brossez vos

    c/ vous rasez les

    d/ vous brosser

10/ Tu _____ beaucoup à la plage.

    a/ s'amusent

    b/ s'amusent

    c/ t'amuses

    d/ s'amuser

11/ Ils _____ tous les jours.

    a/ se dispute

    b/ se disputent

    c/ se disputer

    d/ disputent

12/ Ma grand-mère _____ souvent de numéro de téléphone.

a/ se tromper
b/ se trompent
c/ se trompe
d/ trompe

13/ Ma cousine et moi, nous _____ tous les jours.

a/ nous parlons
b/ nous parlent
c/ nous parler
d/ vous parler

14/ Marc et Sophie _____samedi. Leur mariage est dimanche.

a/ se marier
b/ ne pas se marier
c/ ne se marie pas
d/ ne se marient pas

15/ Elle est fatiguée. Elle_____.

a/ va me coucher
b/ va coucher
c/ va se coucher
d/ aller coucher

16/ J'ai mal à la tête. Je _____bien.

a/ ne me sens pas
b/ ne sens pas
c/ ne pas sentir
d/ sens

17/ Elle _____ toujours le prénom des gens.

a/ ne pas se rappeler
b/ ne pas se rappeler
c/ ne te rappelle pas
d/ ne se rappelle pas

18/ Les étudiants _____ d'arriver en retard.

a/ s'excuse
b/ t'excuses
c/ s'excusent
d/ s'excuser

19/ Elle _____ souvent pendant le cours de biologie.

a/ s'ennuie
b/ s'ennuyer
c/ t'ennuies
d/ ennuie

20/ Vous _____ toujours le prénom des gens.

a/ vous rappeler
b/ vous rappelez
c/ rappelle
d/ se rappelle

21/ Elle _____ avant d'aller à la fête.

a/ maquille
b/ se maquille
c/ se maquiller
d/ maquillée

22/ Nous _____ après la réunion.

a/ nous réunissons
b/ nous réunir
c/ nous réunissez
d/ se réunir

23/ Je _____ deux fois par jour.

a/ se doucher
b/ se douche
c/ me doucher
d/ me douche

24/ Charles et Marie, _____ depuis longtemps ?

a/ s'aimer
b/ s'aiment-ils
c/ aiment-ils
d/ sont aimés

25/ Carolina, tu _____ pour cet examen.

a/ ne t'es pas préparée
b/ te préparer
c/ ne t'es pas préparé
d/ ne pas préparer

RÉPONSES :

1/b	6/a	11/b	16/a	21/b
2/d	7/c	12/c	17/d	22/a
3/b	8/a	13/a	18/c	23/d
4/d	9/a	14/d	19/a	24/b
5/d	10/c	15/c	20/b	25/a

SCORE : _____/25

NOTES :

CHAPITRE 12

Les comparatifs

Choisissez la bonne réponse :

1/ La pizza est _____ que le brocoli.

    a/ meilleur
    b/ meilleure
    c/ bon
    d/ bonne

2/ Marianne est _____ que son frère.

    a/ plus gentille
    b/ la plus gentille
    c/ le plus gentil
    d/ plus gentil

3/ Sarah a _____ que son cousin.

    a/ le plus d'argent
    b/ autant argent
    c/ autant de
    d/ autant d'argent

4/ Il court _____ que son concurrent.

    a/ plus rapide
    b/ plus vite
    c/ le plus
    d/ le plus vite

5/ Le test est _____ que l'examen.

    a/ aussi difficile
    b/ le moins difficile
    c/ difficile
    d/ autant difficile

6/ Il a _____ que son neveu.

    a/ le moins de livres
    b/ moins que les livres
    c/ moins de livres
    d/ moins

7/ Je cuisine _____ que ma mère.

    a/ plus de
    b/ plus souvent
    c/ souvent plus de
    d/ assez souvent

8/ Il a _____ jouets que son petit frère.

    a/ autant
    b/ aussi
    c/ autant de
    d/ autant que

9/ Sa maison est _____ que leur appartement.

    a/ plus cher
    b/ chère
    c/ le plus
    d/ plus chère

10/ J'ai _____ chance que toi.

    a/ moins de
    b/ moins
    c/ la moins
    d/ moins que

11/ Ce steak est _____ que cette omelette.

    a/ plus cuite
    b/ plus cuit
    c/ plus
    d/ plus de

12/ Sonia dort _____ sa grande sœur.

a/ moins que
b/ moins de
c/ le moins
d/ moins

13/ Ta mère pilote_____ un hélicoptère que ta tante.

a/ meilleur
b/ meilleure
c/ mieux
d/ le mieux

14/ Nous buvons _____ café que vous.

a/ plus de
b/ plus que
c/ de plus
d/ le plus

15/ Elle travaille _____ bien que ses copines.

a/ le moins
b/ moins
c/ moins que
d/ moins de

16/ Il a _____ jeux vidéo que son frère.

a/ autant
b/ aussi
c/ autant de
d/ aussi de

17/ Tu fais _____ le café que ton mari.

a/ mieux
b/ le mieux
c/ bien
d/ bien de

18/ Tes cousines sont _____ que tes nièces.

    a/ plus grands
    b/ plus grandes
    c/ aussi grands
    d/ moins grands

19/ Il y a _____ tables dans ce restaurant.

    a/ plus que
    b/ plus
    c/ plus de
    d/ de plus

20/ Le petit garçon dort _____ que la petite fille.

    a/ plus longtemps
    b/ plus long
    c/ plus longue
    d/ le plus longtemps

21/ Cette lampe éclaire _____ que ce spot lumineux.

    a/ meilleur
    b/ meilleure
    c/ mieux
    d/ le mieux

22/ Le vélo est un _____ exercice que la marche.

    a/ meilleur
    b/ mieux
    c/ meilleure
    d/ bien

23/ Cette actrice a _____ admirateurs que cet acteur.

    a/ moins de
    b/ moins d'
    c/ moins que
    d/ le moins

24/ Ils sont _____ que leurs collègues.

    a/ plus travailleur
    b/ plus travailleuses
    c/ plus travailleurs
    d/ plus que travailleurs

25/ Ce croissant est _____ que cette brioche.

    a/ moins croustillant
    b/ moins croustillante
    c/ le moins croustillant
    d/ la moins croustillante

RÉPONSES:

1/b	6/c	11/b	16/c	21/c
2/a	7/b	12/a	17/a	22/a
3/d	8/c	13/c	18/b	23/b
4/b	9/d	14/a	19/c	24/c
5/a	10/a	15/b	20/a	25/a

SCORE : _____/25

NOTES :

CHAPITRE 13

Les superlatifs

Choisissez la bonne réponse :

1/ C'est _____ chanson de l'année.

    a/ la meilleure
    b/ le meilleur
    c/ meilleure
    d/ meilleur

2/ Cécile est _____ de volley-ball de l'équipe.

    a/ le pire joueur
    b/ la pire joueuse
    c/ mauvaise joueuse
    d/ pire joueuse

3/ C'est la moto _____ du magasin.

    a/ plus chère
    b/ le plus cher
    c/ la plus chère
    d/ plus cher

4/ Françoise porte _____ robe ce soir.

    a/ le plus beau
    b/ plus belle que
    c/ plus beau
    d/ la plus belle

5/ Ce restaurant est _____ de la région.

    a/ plus connu
    b/ le plus connu
    c/ plus connue
    d/ la plus connue

6/ De tous les chanteurs ici, c'est Bernard qui chante_____.

a/ le meilleur
b/ le mal
c/ le bien
d/ le mieux

7/ C'est _____ réforme de ce gouvernement.

a/ le pire
b/ les pire
c/ la pire
d/ pire

8/ La famille Durand est _____ accueillante du quartier.

a/ le plus
b/ les plus
c/ la plus
d/ les plus

9/ Ma sœur est l'étudiante _____ de la classe.

a/ la plus sérieuse
b/ le plus sérieux
c/ le moins sérieux
d/ plus sérieuse

10/ C'est Sophie qui a gagné _____ matchs.

a/ le moins
b/ de moins
c/ le moins de
d/ le moins que

11/ C'est l'actrice _____ célèbre du monde.

a/ le plus
b/ les plus
c/ de plus
d/ la plus

12/ Elle préfère acheter _____ gâteau pour ses enfants.

a/ plus gros
b/ plus gros que
c/ la plus grosse
d/ le plus gros

13/ Nous nous baignons dans _____ lac de la région.

a/ la plus grande
b/ le plus grand
c/ plus grand
d/ plus grande

14/ Son chat est _____ de tous ses animaux domestiques.

a/ les plus gentils
b/ le plus gentil
c/ la plus gentille
d/ plus gentil que

15/ C'est la destination _____ exotique du monde.

a/ les plus
b/ le plus
c/ la plus
d/ plus de

16/ Ce site internet est _____ de l'année.

a/ plus populaire que
b/ plus populaires
c/ la plus populaire
d/ le plus populaire

17/ Cette chanson est _____ de l'album de ce chanteur.

a/ la meilleure
b/ le meilleur
c/ meilleur que
d/ le mieux

18/ Pour beaucoup de gens, les chiens sont les animaux _____.

a/ le plus fidèle
b/ la plus fidèle
c/ les plus fidèles
d/ plus fidèles

19/ Le monument _____ de la ville se trouve dans la vieille ville.

a/ le plus visité
b/ la plus visitée
c/ plus visitée
d/ plus visitée que

20/ L'émission de télévision _____ est sur la chaîne 54.

a/ le plus regardé
b/ plus regardé que
c/ plus regardée
d/ la plus regardée

21/ Cette recette de cuisine est _____.

a/ le plus délicieux
b/ la plus délicieuse
c/ délicieuse que
d/ moins délicieuse

22/ Le stylo rouge est le stylo qui écrit _____.

a/ la mieux
b/ mieux
c/ moins bien
d/ le mieux

23/ Cette photo est _____ de l'exposition.

a/ la plus belle
b/ le plus beau
c/ les plus beaux
d/ les plus belles

24/ Cette maison est _____ du village.

    a/ le plus ancien
    b/ la plus ancienne
    c/ moins ancienne
    d/ le moins ancien

25/ Je voudrais réserver l'appartement _____ de l'immeuble.

    a/ moins moderne
    b/ plus moderne
    c/ la plus moderne
    d/ le plus moderne

RÉPONSES:

1/a	6/d	11/d	16/d	21/b
2/b	7/c	12/d	17/a	22/d
3/c	8/c	13/b	18/c	23/a
4/d	9/a	14/b	19/a	24/b
5/b	10/c	15/c	20/d	25/d

SCORE : _____ /25

NOTES :

CHAPITRE 14

Le présent

Choisissez la bonne réponse :

1/ Vous _____ vos devoirs.

a/ fait
b/ faites
c/ faisons
d/ fais

2/ Nous _____ conduire toute la nuit.

a/ doive
b/ devoir
c/ devons
d/ dois

3/ Elle _____ ses amis.

a/ attends
b/ attend
c/ attendent
d/ attendons

4/ Je ne _____ pas cette leçon.

a/ comprends
b/ comprend
c/ comprendre
d/ comprenne

5/ Nous _____ la chambre de notre fille.

a/ peint
b/ peins
c/ peinte
d/ peignons

6/ Nous _____ un bateau qui arrive.

    a/ voir
    b/ voient
    c/ voyons
    d/ vois

7/ Vous _____ un roman toutes les semaines.

    a/ lis
    b/ lisez
    c/ lit
    d/ lisons

8/ Tu _____ la physique et la chimie.

    a/ études
    b/ étudies
    c/ étudie
    d/ étudient

9/ Mes parents _____ des invités à dîner.

    a/ reçoit
    b/ reçois
    c/ recevons
    d/ reçoivent

10/ Tu _____ une robe pour la fête.

    a/ essaies
    b/ essayent
    c/ essayer
    d/ essaie

11/ Vous _____ de lire le roman.

    a/ finissons
    b/ finit
    c/ finissez
    d/ fini

12/ Tu _____ la fenêtre.

a/ ouvrir
b/ ouvres
c/ ouvrez
d/ s'ouvrir

13/ Il _____ de soif.

a/ mort
b/ mourons
c/ meurs
d/ meurt

14/ Elles _____ des fleurs dans un vase.

a/ mettent
b/ mets
c/ mette
d/ mettons

15/ Aujourd'hui, nous _____ des lettres à nos cousines.

a/ écrire
b/ écrivez
c/ écrivons
d/ écririons

16/ Vous _____ la vérité au policier.

a/ dis
b/ dites
c/ disons
d/ direz

17/ Mes amies _____ dans le sud de la France.

a/ voyage
b/ voyages
c/ voyagent
d/ voyagez

18/ Ma sœur _____ nous voir le weekend.

a/ vienne
b/ vient
c/ viens
d/ venir

19/ Elle _____ dans le nord de la France.

a/ vive
b/ vis
c/ vie
d/ vit

20/ Nous _____ une chambre double.

a/ choisissons
b/ choisissez
c/ choisis
d/ choisi

21/ Je _____ avec des amies le mardi soir.

a/ sortons
b/ sort
c/ sorti
d/ sors

22/ Vous _____ qu'elle aime dessiner.

a/ croyons
b/ croit
c/ crois
d/ croyez

23/ Tu _____ la voiture de ton père.

a/ conduis
b/ conduit
c/ conduisez
d/ conduire

24/ Nous _____ dans la chambre du rez-de-chaussée.

a/ dormes
b/ dormons
c/ dort
d/ dormi

25/ Elles _____ la tante de mon meilleur ami.

a/ connaisse
b/ connaît
c/ connaisse
d/ connaissent

RÉPONSES :

1/b	6/c	11/c	16/b	21/d
2/c	7/b	12/b	17/c	22/d
3/b	8/b	13/d	18/b	23/a
4/a	9/d	14/a	19/d	24/b
5/d	10/a	15/c	20/a	25/d

SCORE : _____ **/25**

NOTES :

CHAPITRE 15

L'impératif

Choisissez la bonne réponse :

1/ _____au supermarché avec ta sœur.
  a/ Vas
  b/ Va
  c/ Aller
  d/ Allé

2/ _____ Madame, s'il vous plaît.
  a/ Assieds-toi
  b/ S'asseoir
  c/ Asseyons-nous
  d/ Asseyez-vous

3/ _____ du chocolat chaud si tu as froid.
  a/ Buvez
  b/ Boire
  c/ Buvons
  d/ Bois

4/ Les enfants, _____ attention en jouant dans la rue.
  a/ fait
  b/ faites
  c/ faire
  d/ fasse

5/ _____ rendez-vous chez le dentiste si tu as mal aux dents.
  a/ Prends
  b/ Prendre
  c/ Prend
  d/ Prennent

6/ _____ patient, s'il vous plaît. C'est bientôt votre tour.

a/ Est
b/ Soyez
c/ Sois
d/ Soient

7/ Tu as l'air fatigué. _____ avant de voyager ce soir.

a/ Reposez
b/ Repose
c/ Repose-toi
d/ Se reposer

8/ _____ peur. Mon chien est très gentil.

a/ N'aie pas
b/ Ne pas avoir
c/ N'ayez
d/ Ayez

9/ _____ votre dessert pour que je vous apporte votre café.

a/ Finir
b/ Finis
c/ Finissez
d/ Finit

10/ _____ à notre grand-mère pour son anniversaire.

a/ Écrire
b/ Écrit
c/ Écrivent
d/ Écrivons

11/ _____ ici, s'il te plaît. Je reviens dans cinq minutes.

a/ Attends
b/ Attendons
c/ Attend
d/ Attendre

12/ _____ pour moi et je te rembourserai demain.

a/ Payer
b/ Paient
c/ Paies
d/ Paie

13/ Marie, _____ le premier paragraphe de ce texte.

a/ Lisent
b/ Lis
c/ Lit
d/ Lire

14/ _____ me suivre, s'il vous plaît. Votre table est prête.

a/ Voulez
b/ Veut
c/ Veux
d/ Veuillez

15/ _____ ta mère sinon elle va s'inquiéter.

a/ Appeler
b/ Appelles
c/ Appelle
d/ Appellent

RÉPONSES :

1/b	6/b	11/a
2/d	7/c	12/d
3/d	8/a	13/b
4/b	9/c	14/d
5/a	10/d	15/c

SCORE : _____ **/15**

NOTES :

CHAPITRE 16

Le passé composé

Choisissez la bonne réponse :

1/ Le chauffeur _____ les valises.
   a/ à porter
   b/ a porté
   c/ as porté
   d/ avez porté

2/ Les enfants _____ le match de tennis.
   a/ a regardé
   b/ avons regardé
   c/ sont regardés
   d/ ont regardé

3/ Elles _____ de l'aéroport.
   a/ sommes revenus
   b/ sont revenus
   c/ sont revenues
   d/ être revenu

4/ Est-ce que tu _____ le journal ?
   a/ as lu
   b/ a lu
   c/ ai lu
   d/ est lu

5/ La tarte aux fraises qu'elle _____ est excellente.
   a/ a fait
   b/ avoir fait
   c/ à faire
   d/ a faite

6/ Ta copine et sa mère_____ très tard hier soir.

a/ ont rentré
b/ a rentré
c/ êtes rentrés
d/ sont rentrées

7/ Il _____ trois litres d'eau dans la journée.

a/ ont bu
b/ a bu
c/ as bu
d/ à boire

8/ Sophie _____ à l'université à Toulouse.

a/ est parti
b/ est partie
c/ es parti
d/ es partie

9/ Sophie et Robert _____ heureux de leur concert.

a/ sont sortis
b/ sommes sorties
c/ sommes sortis
d/ sont sorties

10/ Notre voisine _____ dans un accident de voiture.

a/ être morte
b/ mourir
c/ est morte
d/ est mort

11/ Elle _____ au premier étage.

a/ est montée
b/ es monté
c/ es montée
d/ suis montée

12/ Tu _____ repartir au bureau.

    a/ avez dû
    b/ a dû
    c/ à devoir
    d/ as dû

13/ Elle _____ répondre à toutes les questions.

    a/ à savoir
    b/ a su
    c/ ont su
    d/ as su

14/ Ils _____ à Tokyo pendant des années.

    a/ ont vécu
    b/ a vécu
    c/ avons vécu
    d/ à vivre

15/ Elle _____ deux semaines.

    a/ est resté
    b/ est restée
    c/ sont restées
    d/ restée

RÉPONSES :

1/b	6/d	11/a
2/d	7/b	12/d
3/c	8/b	13/b
4/a	9/a	14/a
5/d	10/c	15/b

SCORE : _____ **/15**

NOTES :

CHAPITRE 17

L'imparfait

Choisissez la bonne réponse :

1/ Il _____ au lycée en Bretagne.
a/ allions
b/ allait
c/ allaient
d/ irait

2/ Quand il _____ petit, il _____ au ping-pong.
a/ étais/jouais
b/ étaient/jouait
c/ était/jouaient
d/ était/jouait

3/ Il _____ très beau hier.
a/ faisait
b/ faisais
c/ fait
d/ faire

4/ Quand il est arrivé, elle _____ son cours de physique.
a/ révisait
b/ révisiez
c/ révisaient
d/ révisais

5/ Nous _____ nos vacances à la montagne.
a/ passions
b/ passiez
c/ passer
d/ passaient

6/ Tu _____ des romans policiers dans ton enfance.

a/ lisait
b/ lecture
c/ lisais
d/ lire

7/ J'_____ raison hier et tu _____ tort.

a/ avais/avais
b/ avais/avait
c/ avait/avais
d/ avait/avait

8/ Nous _____ nos grands-parents tous les étés.

a/ voyons
b/ voyaient
c/ voyions
d/ voyiez

9/ Quand vous _____ jeune, vous _____ des cartes postales.

a/ étiez/envoyait
b/ étiez/envoyiez
c/ étais/envoyiez
d/ étiez/envoyez

10/ Ils ne _____ pas que c'_____ possible.

a/ croyait/était
b/ croyais/étais
c/ croyais/étais
d/ croyaient/était

11/ Vous _____ trop vite sur l'autoroute.

a/ conduisiez
b/ conduisait
c/ conduisez
d/ conduire

12/ Nous _____ du lait avec du chocolat.

a/ buvons
b/ buvions
c/ buvais
d/ buvait

13/ Vous _____ en anglais à toutes les questions.

a/ répondez
b/ répondais
c/ répondiez
d/ répondaient

14/ Dans ma jeunesse, nous _____ des romans du Moyen-Âge.

a/ étudiions
b/ étudions
c/ étudiez
d/ étudiaient

15/ Il _____ son repas quand elles _____.

a/ finissais/sont arrivées
b/ finissaient/sont arrivés
c/ finissait/ arrivait
d/ finissait/sont arrivées

RÉPONSES :

1/b	6/c	11/a
2/d	7/a	12/b
3/a	8/c	13/c
4/a	9/b	14/a
5/a	10/d	15/d

SCORE : _____/15

NOTES :

CHAPITRE 18

Le futur proche & le futur simple

Choisissez la bonne réponse :

1/ Elle _____ un nouvel ordinateur demain.

   a/ va nous donner
   b/ aller nous donner
   c/ vont nous donner
   d/ vas nous donner

2/ Nous _____ faire une randonnée.

   a/ irai
   b/ iront
   c/ irons
   d/ iras

3/ Nous _____ au mariage.

   a/ allons assister
   b/ allez assister
   c/ aller assister
   d/ venir assister

4/ Tu _____ plus de chance la prochaine fois.

   a/ avoir
   b/ aura
   c/ auras
   d/ iras

5/ Il _____ à la réunion un peu plus tard.

   a/ venir
   b/ viendra
   c/ viendras
   d/ à venir

6/ Vous _____ accepté dans ce programme.

a/ allez être
b/ aller être
c/ être allé
d/ allé être

7/ Nous vous _____ votre commande demain.

a/ envoyons
b/ enverra
c/ enverrons
d/ envoyer

8/ Il _____ couper cette pizza en six parts.

a/ vouloir
b/ voudra
c/ voudrai
d/ voudrez

9/ Tu _____ ton colis mardi.

a/ recevront
b/ recevrai
c/ recevoir
d/ recevras

10/ Vous _____ garer votre voiture dans le parking.

a/ devoir
b/ doit
c/ devez
d/ devrez

11/ Il _____ nous conduire à la gare.

a/ peux
b/ pouvez
c/ pourra
d/ pouvoir

12/ Ce restaurant _____ dans une semaine.

  a/ fermera
  b/ fermer
  c/ fermé
  d/ fermerai

13/ Elle _____ la direction du cabinet médical de son père.

  a/ va reprendre bientôt
  b/ va bientôt reprendre
  c/ bientôt va reprendre
  d/ bientôt reprendre

14/ Je _____ ce roman pendant mes vacances.

  a/ lire
  b/ lira
  c/ lirai
  d/ lirez

15/ Demain je te _____ tes livres de français.

  a/ donnera
  b/ donnerai
  c/ donnerais
  d/ donneriez

RÉPONSES :

1/a	6/a	11/c
2/c	7/c	12/a
3/a	8/b	13/b
4/c	9/d	14/c
5/b	10/d	15/b

SCORE : _____ /15

NOTES :

CHAPITRE 19

Le conditionnel

Choisissez la bonne réponse :

1/ Tu _____voyager plus souvent.

a/ devraient
b/ devrais
c/ devrait
d/ devais

2/ Nous _____ faire un cadeau à notre grand-mère.

a/ aimerions
b/ aimerait
c/ aimerait
d/ aimeraient

3/ _____ -vous m'aider à trouver le bureau de poste ?

a/ Pouvons
b/ Pourrais
c/ Pourriez
d/ Pourrai

4/ Je _____ acheter un billet pour Paris.

a/ voudrions
b/ voudraient
c/ voudrait
d/ voudrais

5/ Tu _____ si je t'expliquais.

a/ comprendraient
b/ comprendrais
c/ comprendre
d/ comprendrions

6/ Elle _____ faire cette équation si tu lui expliquais.

a/ serait
b/ saurait
c/ saurais
d/ sauraient

7/ J'ai entendu dire qu'elle _____ de la famille au Canada.

a/ aurait
b/ auraient
c/ auriez
d/ avoir

8/ Il était sûr qu'elle _____ à son histoire.

a/ croirais
b/ croire
c/ croirait
d/ croiriez

9/ Je me demande si tu ne_____ pas mieux avec des lunettes.

a/ verraient
b/ verrait
c/ verrais
d/ voyait

10/ Nous _____ heureux de vous voir.

a/ serions
b/ serait
c/ être
d/ serais

11/ Je _____ bien en montgolfière une fois dans ma vie.

a/ voyager
b/ voyagerais
c/ voyagerait
d/ voyagerai

12/ Si tu regardais mieux, tu _____ les lapins dans le jardin.

a/ apercevoir
b/ apercevra
c/ apercevait
d/ apercevrais

13/ Nous _____ vous inviter à notre mariage.

a/ voudrions
b/ voudrons
c/ voudriez
d/ voudrait

14/ Elle t'_____ une lettre si elle avait ton adresse.

a/ enverrez
b/ enverrais
c/ envoie
d/ enverrait

15/ _____ - tu si nous t'invitions ?

a/ Viendrais
b/ Viendriez
c/ Viendront
d/ Viendraient

RÉPONSES :

1/b	6/b	11/b
2/a	7/a	12/d
3/c	8/c	13/a
4/d	9/c	14/d
5/b	10/a	15/a

SCORE : _____/15

NOTES :

CHAPITRE 20

Test diagnostique

Choisissez la bonne réponse :

1/ Elle _____ nous apporter de cadeau.
  a/ ne va pas
  b/ ne pas aller
  c/ ne va
  d/ ne vais pas

2/ Le lapin _____ dans le jardin.
  a/ est sortie
  b/ est sorti
  c/ à sortir
  d/ es sorti

3/ Nous _____ dans une heure.
  a/ arriverons
  b/ arrivera
  c/ aller arriver
  d/ arriverait

4/ Il achète _____ café et _____ confiture.
  a/ du/du
  b/ de la/de la
  c/ de/de la
  d/ du/de la

5/ _____ fais-tu ? Je fais mes devoirs.
  a/ Qui
  b/ Quoi
  c/ Qu'est-ce qui
  d/ Que

6/ Il _____ en vacances en Bretagne quand il était petit.

a/ allait
b/ va
c/ à aller
d/ ira

7/ _____ ordinateur est bon marché.

a/ Cette
b/ C'est
c/ Cet
d/ Ces

8/ Vous _____ dans la chambre 12.

a/ ira
b/ irez
c/ irons
d/ allaient aller

9/ _____ est un excellent médecin.

a/ Cet
b/ Il
c/ Cette
d/ C'

10/ _____ amis arriveront vers huit heures.

a/ Mon
b/ Ma
c/ Mes
d/ Mais

11/ Tu vas au cinéma ? Oui, j'_____ vais.

a/ y
b/ le
c/ lui
d/ en

12/ Ils _____ déjeuner dans la cuisine.

a/ peux
b/ peuvent
c/ peut
d/ pouvons

13/ Parlez-vous à <u>vos grands-parents</u> ? Oui, nous _____ parlons.

a/ lui
b/ leur
c/ les
d/ leurs

14/ Les chiens _____ toute la journée.

a/ ont dormi
b/ a dormi
c/ à dormir
d/ avez dormi

15/ Paris est _____ ville du monde.

a/ le plus beau
b/ moins belle
c/ plus beau
d/ la plus belle

16/ On construit un _____ hôpital dans la ville.

a/ nouvelle
b/ nouveau
c/ nouvel
d/ nouveaux

17/ Les _____ sont _____.

a/ manteau/neufs
b/ manteaux/ neuf
c/ manteaux/neufs
d/ manteaux/neuves

18/ Elles _____ tôt pour aller travailler hier.

a/ se sont réveillés
b/ se sont réveillées
c/ se réveillent
d/ se réveiller

19/ La table est _____ que les chaises

a/ plus grand
b/ plus grandes
c/ la plus grande
d/ plus grande

20/ Mange-t-elle du pain ? Oui, elle _____ mange.

a/ en
b/ y
c/ le
d/ la

21/ Ils _____ un film de science-fiction.

a/ verront
b/ verra
c/ verrai
d/ voir

22/ _____ robe va bien avec _____ jupe.

a/ Cette/cet
b/ Cet/cette
c/ Cette/cette
d/ Ce/cet

23/ _____ tu attends ? J'attends le bus.

a/ Est-ce que
b/ Quoi
c/ Qu'est-ce que
d/ Où

24/ Ils _____ chez nous pendant deux semaines.

a/ est resté
b/ sont restés
c/ sommes restés
d/ sont restées

25/ Vas-tu toujours à <u>la piscine</u> ? Oui, j'_____vais toujours.

a/ en
b/ y
c/ le
d/ lui

26/ Nous allons _____ plage _____ Espagne.

a/ au/en
b/ à la/au
c/ au/au
d/ à la/en

27/ Vous _____ marié et vous _____ deux enfants.

a/ êtes/avez
b/ êtes/a
c/ est/avez
d/ êtes/suis

28/ _____ étudiante et _____ professeurs sont dans la classe.

a/ La/les
b/ L'/le
c/ Le/les
d/ L'/les

29/ Les fauteuils sont _____ que les chaises.

a/ plus confortable
b/ confortables
c/ plus confortables
d/ plus que

30/ Ce sont les vélos de Pierre. Ce sont _____ vélos.

a/ ses
b/ mes
c/ leurs
d/ tes

31/ Est-ce que tu _____ déjà travailler ?

a/ pars
b/ partir
c/ part
d/ partez

32/ Ce jardin est _____ du quartier.

a/ la plus grande
b/ plus grand
c/ le plus grand
d/ plus grand que

33/ _____ vas-tu payer l'addition ? Avec une carte de crédit.

a/ Combien
b/ Comment
c/ À qui
d/ Quoi

34/ _____ quelle heure te réveilles-tu le matin ?

a/ Pour
b/ De
c/ À
d/ Par

35/ J'écris à <u>mes cousins</u>. Je _____ écris.

a/ lui
b/ les
c/ leurs
d/ leur

36/ _____ enfants jouent ensemble à l'école.

a/ Leur
b/ Leurs
c/ Le
d/ De

37/ _____ portes-tu un tee-shirt ? Parce que j'ai chaud.

a/ Pourquoi
b/ Comment
c/ Combien
d/ Où

38/ Qui va faire un gâteau ? Sophie _____.

a/ va faire un
b/ va le faire
c/ va lui faire
d/ va en faire un

39/ La _____ amie de Carla est _____.

a/ nouvelle/gentille
b/ nouvel/gentille
c/ nouvelle/gentil
d/ nouvel/gentille

40/ Hier, mes deux sœurs _____ se promener.

a/ sont allés
b/ vont aller
c/ sont allées
d/ être et aller

41/ Ta maison est _____ que mon chalet.

a/ moins de
b/ moins vieux
c/ moins vieil
d/ moins vieille

42/ Tes parents ? Je _____ aime beaucoup.

a/ eux

b/ leur

c/ les

d/ lui

43/ Tu manges _____ poisson mais pas _____ viande.

a/ de la/de

b/ du/de la

c/ de la/de

d/ du/de

44/ Ma grand-mère est _____ et _____.

a/ canadienne/sportive

b/ canadien/sportive

c/ canadienne/sportif

d/ canadien/sportif

45/ Tu joues encore au football ? Non, je _____ au football.

a/ ne joue pas

b/ ne joue plus

c/ joue pas

d/ joue toujours

46/ _____ ! Tu vas être en retard !

a/ Réveillez

b/ Réveille-moi

c/ Réveille-toi

d/ Se réveiller

47/ Nous habitons en Alsace _____ trois ans.

a/ depuis

b/ pendant

c/ en

d/ dans

48/ J'_____ trois films dans la journée.

a/ ai vu
b/ avez vu
c/ as vu
d/ avoir vu

49/ Londres a _____ que Paris.

a/ parcs
b/ plus de
c/ plus de parcs
d/ des parcs

50/ À 10 ans, j'_____ l'habitude de manger beaucoup de chocolat.

a/ avais
b/ avait
c/ avoir
d/ avez eu

RÉPONSES :

1/a	11/a	21/a	31/a	41/d
2/b	12/b	22/c	32/c	42/c
3/a	13/b	23/c	33/b	43/d
4/d	14/a	24/b	34/c	44/a
5/d	15/d	25/b	35/d	45/b
6/a	16/c	26/d	36/b	46/c
7/c	17/c	27/a	37/a	47/a
8/b	18/b	28/d	38/d	48/a
9/d	19/d	29/c	39/a	49/c
10/c	20/a	30/a	40/c	50/a

SCORE: _____ /50

NOTES :

ABOUT THE
AUTHOR

Born in Versailles and raised in Paris, Véronique graduated from Paris-III Sorbonne Nouvelle (B.A. in English/M.A. in American Studies) while working for an American Junior Year Abroad Program in Paris. She went on to teach French Culture and Cinema at Tufts University and Boston University for 15 years. She graduated from the School of Communications at Boston University (M.S. in Advertising & Public Relations).

Shortly after graduating from UCLA with a Certificate in Film Distribution & Marketing, she worked for several film distribution companies.

In 2004, she founded her own film distribution company, Casque d'or films. In 2008, she wrote and directed an animated short film that premiered at the AFI Film Festival in Los Angeles. In 2010, she wrote and directed an animated short series entitled THE QUEER PET ADVENTURES. Both titles screened at many film festivals worldwide and are currently distributed in French and German territories.

Since settling in Los Angeles, she has also worked as a French Instructor at the Beverly Hills Lingual Institute and has taught language seminars at the Alliance Française of Los Angeles.

Her first published novel, written in French, is entitled, The Parisian Adventures of Kimberly. It is a French Reader, a novel intended to help intermediate learners of French to review the language in an entertaining and relaxed way. The book is part of a three-book set, composed of the novel written in French, the Activity Book that includes a wide variety of French vocabulary practice exercises, and the Answer key that provides answers to all the exercises.

Véronique just completed her second French Reader entitled Treasure in Occitania. She is also working on two other novels and two English to French Translation Workbooks for intermediate and advanced learners of French. Besides writing, she is currently training as a baker and pastry chef.

CONNECT WITH

VÉRONIQUIE

Facebook Page:
www.facebook.com/VeroniqueFCourtoisBooks

Twitter:
@vfcfrenchauthor

LinkedIn
www.linkedin.com/in/veronique-courtois-72486616

SoundCloud
www.soundcloud.com/user-165718002

DEAR READER...

Thank you for purchasing my books! I hope you're enjoying or enjoyed reading them.

As a bilingual writer, I always seek to write stories that will interest my readers and allow them to become more familiar with the French language and culture. So I would mostly welcome your suggestions and I'd be very grateful for the lovely comments! I'd be delighted if you could leave an honest review on Amazon as well. I love reading reviews for my books.

To leave a review, your can either search *The Ultimate French Quiz Book for Beginner & Intermediate Levels* by Véronique F. Courtois on Amazon, click the book and leave a review

Or you could email me at **vfcfrenchbooks@gmail.com**. I welcome all suggestions and comments.

Thank you again for your interest. Keep learning French!

OTHER BOOKS BY

VÉRONIQUIE

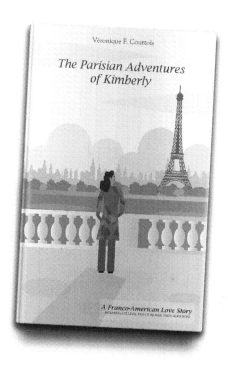

**The Parisian Adventures of Kimberly
(Les Aventures Parisiennes de Kimberly):
A Franco-American Love Story**

A perfect French for students book! This story has been made easier to understand by dividing each of the chapters into three parts. Key vocabulary has been highlighted, and the corresponding translations can be found in a box right beneath each section. This will provide you, the reader, with immediate support, and will help to ensure a great learning experience.

Activity Book for
The Parisian Adventures of Kimberly

This French reader workbook has been written to complement the intermediate level French reader novel entitled The Parisian Adventures of Kimberly by Véronique F. Courtois. This book fulfills a double purpose: Practicing reading comprehension and review vocabulary through a large variety of French reading exercises.

Answer Key to the Activity Book for
The Parisian Adventures of Kimberly

This Answer Key book provides Intermediate French learners with the answers to reading comprehension questions, translation exercises and a wide variety of vocabulary exercises included in the Activity Book for The Parisian Adventures of Kimberly: Intermediate Level French Reader that supports B1, B2, and C1 levels of French proficiency.

Check out the series on Amazon:
www.amazon.com/gp/product/B084M74WD5

Printed in Great Britain
by Amazon